Published by Mz. Kim Productions
4263 Tierra Rejada Rd #151
Moorpark, CA 93021
www.mzkimproductions.com

ISBN: 978-1-962106-07-8

Printed in United States of America
First Printing: August 2023
Date of Copyright: July 5,2023
Cover design by Indalecio Chavez Jr.
Illustrations by Indalecio Chavez Jr.

For permissions, please contact: Mz. Kim Productions
4263 Tierra Rejada Rd #151
Moorpark, CA 93021
www.mzkimproductions.com
mzkimproductions@gmail.com

Dedication:

To my beloved grandmother, Margie, whose love, wisdom, and teachings continue to inspire generations. Thank you for instilling in me the values of faith, kindness, and the importance of following God's commandments. This book is dedicated to you, Grandma Margie, and to all the grandmothers who leave an everlasting impact on their grandchildren's lives. Your love and guidance will forever be cherished.

To my family, who has always been my greatest source of support and encouragement. Thank you for standing by me throughout this journey and for being a constant reminder of the power of love and faith. Your unwavering belief in me has fueled my passion for writing, and I am grateful for each and every one of you.

To the readers of "Grandma Margie's Tale Of The Ten Commandments," thank you for embarking on this enchanting journey with us. It is my hope that this book will not only entertain and inspire your children but also foster meaningful conversations about faith, values, and the importance of living a righteous life. May the lessons within these pages resonate with you and guide you in your own journey.

May this book serve as a reminder that love, kindness, and the Ten Commandments are timeless principles that can enrich our lives and bring us closer to God. May it inspire you to embrace these values and share them with others, creating a ripple effect of goodness and compassion in the world.

With heartfelt gratitude,
Dr. K.T. Zulkowski

Dear Readers,

I am thrilled to present to you "Grandma Margie's Ten Commandments," a book that holds a special place in my heart. As the author, it is my utmost pleasure to share this story with you and your children.

This book was inspired by the love and wisdom of my own grandmother, Grandma Margie, who played a significant role in shaping my values and beliefs. Through her teachings and the lessons she imparted, I have come to appreciate the power of God's commandments in guiding our lives.

"Grandma Margie's Ten Commandments" is not only a story but also a tool for teaching children about moral values, spirituality, and the importance of living a righteous life. It is my hope that this book will inspire meaningful conversations between parents, teachers, and children about the significance of following God's commandments.

Through the characters of Grandma Margie, Zipporah, and Zion, children will learn about the power of love, forgiveness, honesty, and respect. They will understand that these commandments are not merely rules to adhere to, but principles that can enrich their lives and build strong character.

I believe that instilling these values in our children at an early age is crucial for their personal and social development. By teaching them the Ten Commandments, we lay the foundation for them to become compassionate, responsible, and principled individuals.

I hope that "Grandma Margie's Tale Of The Ten Commandments" will not only entertain your children but also serve as a valuable educational resource. May it inspire them to embrace these timeless principles and lead lives that are guided by love, kindness, and righteousness.

With warmest regards,

Dr. K.T. Zulkowski

Educational Value:

"Grandma Margie's Tale Of The Ten Commandments" holds significant educational value for young readers. It introduces children to the biblical principles of the Ten Commandments in a relatable and accessible manner. The book promotes moral and ethical values, such as kindness, forgiveness, honesty, and respect, which are essential for building character and fostering positive relationships. It also encourages children to develop a deeper understanding of their faith and provides a foundation for discussions about spirituality and religious teachings. Through the story's relatable characters and engaging illustrations, children can learn about the practical application of these commandments in their everyday lives. Overall, the book promotes important life lessons and values, making it a valuable educational resource for parents, teachers, and caregivers.

"Grandma Margie's Tale of the Ten Commandments"

Written By Dr. K.T. Zulkowski

Illustrated By Indalecio Chavez Jr.

Once upon a time, my sweet grandchildren, there were some very special rules that God gave us to live by. These rules are called the Ten Commandments.

Can you tell us what the first commandment is, Grandma?

Of course, my dear. The first commandment says, "You shall have no other gods before me." It means that we should love and worship only God.

Grandma, what is the second commandment?

The second commandment says, "You shall not make for yourself an idol." It means we should not worship statues or things like that, but focus on God's love and teachings.

What comes after that, Grandma?

The third commandment says, "You shall not misuse the name of the Lord your God." It means we should always speak God's name with respect and not use it carelessly.

Grandma, what is the fourth commandment?

The fourth commandment says, "Remember the Sabbath day and keep it holy." It means we should set aside one day each week to rest, worship God, and spend time with our loved ones.

What comes after that, Grandma?

The fifth commandment says, "Honor your father and mother." It means we should respect and obey our parents, just as God wants us to.

Grandma, what is the sixth commandment?

The sixth commandment says, "You shall not murder."
It means we should never hurt or harm anyone because
God cherishes all life.

What comes after that, Grandma?

The seventh commandment says,
"You shall not commit adultery."
It means we should be faithful
and true in our relationships,
just as God is faithful to us.

Grandma, what is the eighth commandment?

The eighth commandment says, "You shall not steal." It means we should always respect other people's belongings and never take what is not ours.

What comes after that, Grandma?

The ninth commandment says, "You shall not give false testimony against your neighbor." It means we should always tell the truth and not say things that hurt others.

Grandma, what is the tenth commandment?

The tenth commandment says, "You shall not covet anything that belongs to your neighbor." It means we should be happy with what we have and not be jealous of others.

Now, my little ones, let us pray
and ask God to help us remember and
follow these commandments every day.

Grandma, I want to be good and
follow these commandments!

That's wonderful, my dear! It warms
my heart to hear that. Remember,
following these commandments will lead
us to a life filled with love, peace, and happiness.

Grandma, can we share these commandments with our friends too?

Grandma Margie: Absolutely, my darling! We should always share the love of God and the wisdom of His commandments with everyone we meet.

Grandma, where can we find the Ten Commandments in the Bible?

They can be found in the book of Exodus, chapter 20, my dear. Let's read them together and study God's word.

Grandma, what if we make mistakes and break one of the commandments?

God knows we are not perfect, my sweet boy. When we make mistakes, we can ask God for forgiveness, learn from them, and strive to do better.

Grandma, let's make a promise to always remember and follow the Ten Commandments.

That's a beautiful promise, my darling! Let's hold each other accountable and encourage one another to live by these commandments every day.

Grandma, I want to be like Moses and lead others to a better life through God's commandments.

That's a wonderful aspiration, my brave boy! Just like Moses, you can inspire others to live a life of righteousness and love.

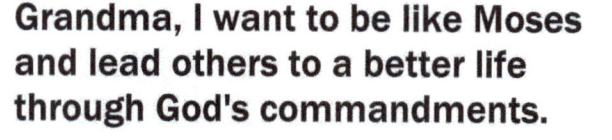

Grandma, thank you for teaching us
about the Ten Commandments.
I feel closer to God now.

You're most welcome, my dear. Remember,
God's commandments are like a roadmap
to guide us on the path of righteousness
and bring us closer to Him.

I will always treasure these commandments in my heart.

And I will always treasure you, my dear grandson.
Keeping God's commandments will bring you joy
and help you live a meaningful and fulfilling life.

Grandma, I want to share
these commandments
with everyone I meet!

That's the spirit, my little ray of
sunshine! By living the commandments
and sharing them with others, we can help
make the world a better place.

My precious grandchildren, always remember that God's love and the commandments are our guiding lights in this journey of life. May they shine brightly in your hearts forever.